Grizzardisms

Grizzardisms

THE WIT AND WISDOM OF LEWIS GRIZZARD

✳

Lewis Grizzard

Villard • New York • 1995

All rights reserved under International and Pan-American
Copyright conventions. Published in the United States by
Villard Books,
a division of Random House, Inc., New York,
and simultaneously in Canada by Random House
of Canada Limited, Toronto.

Villard Books is a registered trademark of
Random House, Inc.

Portions of this book were originally published in *I Took a Lickin' and Kept
on Tickin' (And Now I Believe in Miracles); I Haven't Understood Anything Since
1962 and Other Nekkid Truths; You Can't Put No Boogie-Woogie on the King of
Rock and Roll; If I Ever Get Back to Georgia, I'm Gonna Nail My Feet to the
Ground; Chili Dawgs Always Bark at Night; Don't Bend Over in the Garden,
Granny, You Know Them Taters Got Eyes; When My Love Returns from the Ladies
Room, Will I Be Too Old to Care?;* and *My Daddy Was a Pistol, and I'm a Son of
a Gun,* all by Lewis Grizzard and published by Villard Books, a division of
Random House, Inc., New York, and in Lewis Grizzard's syndicated
newspaper column.

Library of Congress Cataloging-in-Publication Data
Grizzard, Lewis.
Grizzardisms: the wit and wisdom of Lewis Grizzard /
by Lewis Grizzard.
p.   cm.
ISBN 0-679-76895-5
I. Title.
PN6162.G78254   1995
818′.5402—dc20   95-6801

Manufactured in the United States of America on
acid-free paper
9 8 7 6 5 4 3 2
First Edition

For Daddy's little angel

Contents

Grizzardisms

Growing Up

When people ask me what sign I was born under, I say, "I'm not certain, but it could have been the one that says, 'Dining car in the opposite direction.'"

*

The primary reason younger people don't trust older people is because older people sit around and try to figure out how to make life more difficult for younger people than it already is.

*

Kids deserve to win one occasionally.

*

I grew up in a family where water conservation was a way of life. I still cringe when I see pictures of Niagara Falls. The whole thing looks to me like somebody is wasting a lot of good water.

*

I cannot remember my mother ever spending a dime on herself for something she didn't desperately need. I can never remember her buying more than five dollars' worth of gas at a time, either. I think she was afraid if she filled up the tank and died, she would have wasted money on whatever gas remained in her car.

*

Mothers are great, but most of them know little or nothing about basketball.

*

Mothers may not know a lot about basketball, but they do know a lot about little boys' dreams.

*

That's the way we did things back when children still respected their parents and boys didn't wear earrings and nice girls didn't even kiss on the first date and "going all the way" meant a trip to the state capital.

*

One thing I never liked about teachers is they browbeat you with logic.

*

I have been out of high school twenty-four years, and not once has algebra come up.

*

I did like some history, especially the part about George Washington slipping out his window at night during rainstorms in order to rendezvous with one of the slave girls and subsequently catching a cold and dying.

*

Giving freshmen cars would be akin to giving terrorists their own airline.

*

During the oil crunch of the seventies, I thought of all the gasoline we wasted as teenagers driving around the Dairy Queen and figured we probably were the ones who at least started the ball rolling toward an oil crisis.

*

Every time you get behind the wheel of a car, don't try to see how fast the car will go. The morgue is a totally boring place.

*

Unless you've been to a country juke joint on a Saturday night or bass-fished with somebody who knows where the glory holes are, your life is miserably incomplete.

*

Enough years have passed now that I probably could lie about my high school athletic career and get away with most of it.

*

Forty is the year, if you're a single man, it's time you quit messing around with women who don't know how World War II came out.

*

I figure I'll have spent seven years of my life waiting for women to come out of ladies' rooms, eleven years receiving unsolicited advice, eight years watching television (as long as I can still get the Playboy Channel and continue to locate my remote-control device), and two years sitting in traffic. Add all that to the time I'll spend sleeping, and that gives me only a few days left to worry about whether or not the earth is going to get so hot it will burn up.

Writing and Work

I fell in love with newspapers when I was eight because they took me to every minor-league and major-league baseball game.

*

Like all other careers, a writing career actually begins when you begin getting paid.

*

If you work for a morning newspaper, you report in the afternoon and get off when

everybody else is asleep. There are some
good points to these hours. Okay, so I can
think of only *one*: You never have to sit
in traffic.

*

A newspaper is a living, breathing thing,
and to pick up yours as it comes off a press
when it is still warm is to hold
your newborn.

*

Writing a daily newspaper column is like
being married to a nymphomaniac. The first
two weeks, it's fun.

*

I don't think people who deliver the paper get enough credit, quite frankly. I don't care how good the paper is, if the man or woman who is responsible for having it on your lawn—come rain, sleet, snow, or hangover—falters, what difference does it make if four gorillas and an orangutan produce the paper?

*

Four gorillas and an orangutan could put out a better newspaper than the ones some people try to shove down the readers' throats. Most gorillas and orangutans I know at least aren't pinko, left-wing communist bed wetters, which a lot of newspaper people are.

*

Now you have to guess if I'm making this up or not. Being a columnist is great fun.

*

I decided I would become a freelance writer. I didn't know much about how to become a freelance writer, but it is one of those occupations you can go into just by saying you are one. There are a lot of occupations like that. Screenwriters fall into the same category. So do artists, poets,

midnight gynecologists (otherwise known as
"pickup artists"), environmentalists,
adventurers, and political analysts.

*

Some authors, I am told, write out their
books in longhand. That's because they
never learned to type. That's why Edgar
Allan Poe wrote all that weird stuff. His
hands and fingers were always hurting him.
The pain became so intense he began to see
talking ravens.

*

I belong to an idea service. I pay $38.50
twice annually, and a firm in Oregon sends

me an idea for a column four times a week.
For $50 twice annually, I could get good
ideas, but I decided to save my money like
the television networks do when they order
programming ideas.

*

A man should not write the story of his
daddy on anything that has to be
plugged in.

*

I was the first person to interview God. He
said to tell Jimmy Swaggart he was fired.

*

I've talked to two presidents, one man who claimed to be Jesus, and another who said he knew who was buried in the Tomb of the Unknown Soldier but was sworn to secrecy.

*

I hated going into the locker rooms when I was covering sports. They were hot and crowded and smelly, and I could never get used to interviewing large naked men.

*

The sportswriters of today all have college educations, don't get drunk then try to write, actually have read something besides

Sports Illustrated and the Larry Bird autobiography, would rather write about the plantation mentality of big-time college athletic programs than Georgia versus Auburn, are married to women with double last names, drive BMWs, wear shirts that don't have frayed collars, write on a computer rather than a manual typewriter, have no idea who Smoky Burgess was, eat salads for lunch, don't smoke, have never seen *The Babe Ruth Story* starring William Bendix, and have no idea who William Bendix was.

*

I lost Detroit because they hired a new woman editor who canceled my column

because she said I was a sexist. The dumb
broad probably doesn't shave her legs.

*

If I win a Pulitzer, even when my syndicate
calls and says, "Your columns have been a
little stale lately," they'll have to say,
"Your *Pulitzer Prize–winning* columns have
been a little stale lately."

*

Newspapers are the only romance in my life
that hasn't eventually picked up and
left me.

The South

I say if you are going to classes to lose your Southern accent, you are turning your back on your heritage, and I hope you wind up working behind the counter of a convenience store with three Iranians and a former Indian holy man.

*

Who would change your oil and clean out your carburetor if it weren't for straight Southern white males?

*

Southerners can probably say "shit" better than anybody else. We give it the ol' two-syllable "shee-yet," which strings it out a bit and gives it more ambience, if words can have ambience. "Shee-yet far" is Southern for "shit fire," which means something between "Oh my God" and "Look out, Knute, she's headin' for the brier patch."

*

I don't think Southerners actually say "sumbitch." It's more "suhbitch," as in "That suhbitch can flat play a cello," which

I'm not certain has ever been said in the South, but I like to throw in such classy allusions like that to prove we've got more class than Yankees often give us credit for.

*

We don't say "ass" like other people do. I can't decide exactly how we say "ass," but "ice" comes rather close, as in "Shee-yet far, Randy, if that got-damn suhbitch don't watch his ice, somebody's goin' to break that cello right over his got-damn head."

*

Giving Northerners unbuttered instant grits is an old remedy for getting rid of tourists.

It is true I had some relatives who fought
for the South in the Civil War, but they
weren't fighting to save slavery. They were
fighting to make Yankee men dress better
when they visited Southern beaches.

*

Most all straight Southern white males
spend their entire lives trying to avoid
being pissants.

*

Most non-Southerners think men named
Bubba are nothing more than ignorant swine

who wear caps with the names of heavy-
equipment dealers on the front, shoot
anything that moves, listen to music about
doing bodily harm to hippies, and put beer
on their grits.

*

Straight Southern white males—we need
love and understanding, too, and once you
get to know us, we aren't what the cat
drug in from the garbage.

Food

I didn't care if the fact I wouldn't eat liver would cut my life span in half. I reasoned I'd rather live a few good years liverless than a full lifetime of trying to get it down my gullet.

*

In the Old West, they hung out over at the livery stable. Me, I hate liver, but I didn't grow up in the Old West.

*

Today we are urged to eat cereals with names like Nutra-Grain. Isn't that something they feed to cows out in Nebraska?

*

I am by no means obese, but I have noticed my body taking on a different and more rounded shape in an area that may be described as the navel and surrounding areas. It's caused, I think, by fallen chest arches.

*

Drinking alone is bad, but eating alone is worse. You're alone and sober.

*

There were many ethnic restaurants in my rather ethnic neighborhood, but once you've eaten one portion of boiled yak, that's about it for the rest of your life.

*

Anybody who puts sugar in corn bread is a heathen who doesn't love the Lord, not to mention Southeastern Conference football.

＊

Never order barbecue in a place that also serves quiche.

＊

Never order chili in a place where there is a picture of a camel on the menu.

＊

"We always put mushrooms on our cheeseburgers," says my waiter, who has a ponytail and is wearing an earring. Never order a cheeseburger in a place where your waiter thinks he's Gidget.

*

God never intended fried chicken to taste
like some Mexican got loose in the batter
with a pocketful of chili peppers.

Women

I suppose the one thing I've spent the most time trying to figure out since 1962 is why, with the exception of my mother, grandmother, and aunts, I can't get along with women for more than, say, eleven minutes straight.

*

Women: Why don't they have their own damn golf courses.

*

I'm not certain when most women began to
hate most men, but it probably had
something to do with Jane Fonda.

*

If I open a door for a woman, will she take
it to mean I think she's not strong enough
to open it herself and knee me in the groin?

*

Beware of any woman with a hyphenated
last name, expecially if she's your wife's
lawyer in your divorce trial.

*

Your dog won't bring you chicken noodle soup when you're sick, but neither would your last wife, who probably joined a cult of women who worship Cher.

*

When women make up their minds to go, they go.

*

It's been my experience with women that a closet without 416 pairs of shoes in it

is like a necklace with no earrings
to match.

*

I've bought houses in less time than it
takes a woman to shop for a skirt
and blouse.

*

Women think reading a tube of toothpaste
is like reading the Bible. If you don't follow
the instructions on the tube, you will go
to hell.

*

Putting a pair of baggy pants on a woman would be like pulling a shade down over a lovely sunset.

*

The only thing worse than a whiny, pouting woman is a whiny, pouting woman with a flat chest.

*

Women will hang wet panty hose on the shower rod and cover the sink area with an assortment of exotic shampoos and oils, not to mention spare parts for their Volvo station wagons.

*

I've spent what seems like half my life
waiting for some woman to come out of
the ladies' room. Some never came out.
They apparently started new lives for
themselves in there.

*

I honestly think women's liberation has had
a lot to do with men simply saying to
themselves, "I don't need this crap. I'm
never going to find anybody to treat me like
Mama did, so I'll just give up and find me a
good dog."

*

As long as most men can still outrun most women, there's always hope for me.

Love

Monogamy isn't all that bad, once you're used to it. It's safe, it's simple, and you don't have to remember all those names.

*

Let this be a lesson to the young and foolish: Give in to the mad rushes of love! Never hold back when you are filled with the magic of romance! If nothing else works, try a tube of Clearasil!

*

I'd want to point out I'm a dog lover who brushes his teeth regularly, still has his hair, loves egg sandwiches, and often entertains friends by doing a simply marvelous impression of FDR declaring war on the Japanese in 1941. Now, how are you going to get all that in a classified ad?

*

If my social life reaches the desperate point, I can always go after the "SWHWs." Single Waffle House waitresses. They're around twenty-four hours a day and make the best egg sandwiches in town.

*

I despise the word, but I can't remember
what we used to say before we said
"relationship."

*

If you're a straight Southern white male
with an agricultural background, never
marry a former debutante. They don't
know anything about mule farting, which
can create a large gap in the
communications process.

*

The mating call of the Georgia Peach:
"Lordy, I'm sooooo drunk."

*

If you are currently having an affair, you
might want to store this away: All who
cheat eventually get caught. It's God's
way of telling you to find
another hobby.

*

If I ever get married again, I'm going to
suggest separate honeymoons.

Sex

Jokes without sexual overtones are hard to find, and most of them aren't funny.

*

The closest I ever got to group sex was the time Loot Starkins brought two of his sows over to my uncle's farm to have them bred with my uncle's prize boar, Big Jake.

*

There are an awful lot of things that will knock sexuality for a complete loop, and diarrhea ranks right up there.

*

The only chance I'd ever have had of being a homosexual is if I'd been born a girl. As a matter of fact, I'm almost positive I'd've been a lesbian, but I'd have been a picky one. Kim Basinger, yes. Martina Navratilova, absolutely not.

*

You *can* have sex in a roomette on a train hurtling through the Florida night, by the way, but I didn't have the nerve to tell the chiropractor how I actually injured my back.

*

I knew a woman once who was an admitted bisexual. Whoever would buy her things— like a car or jewelry—could be sexual with her.

*

There's nothing inherently dirty about sex, but if you try real hard and use your imagination you can overcome that quite easily.

*

Breasts do not have to come in jumbo size to be pleasing to me, but if I happen to run into a large pair, it's always a joy.

*

I don't care if breasts are store-bought or not. I wore a fake Rolex I bought from a guy on the street corner, and it kept perfect time.

*

It's probably better to involve oneself with a woman who does not have large breasts.

Her alternatives will be greatly diminished compared with large-breasted women, and she will show more gratitude, be more forgiving, and be much more likely to hand-cut her french fries and make you an occasional biscuit from scratch.

*

I have never made it a habit to hang out in nude dancing parlors, but you get to one now and then for bachelor parties, and to celebrate such things as Arizona getting statehood, Grover Cleveland's birthday, Thursday, and making it another day without getting a kidney stone.

*

I am by no means trying to condone adultery, but the fact is, it's one of the most popular of the Ten Commandments to break. Who goes around making graven images today?

Show Biz

One of the problems facing the American male today is his inability to emulate even in the slightest the current movie hero.

*

Remember how cowboys in western movies could get into a fifteen-minute gunfight and never have to reload their pistols?

*

I don't think there is a shred of truth to the rumor that Rhett Butler was actually bisexual and walked out on Scarlett rather than tell her of his true feelings for a certain young Union lieutenant he met at a gay bar Sherman missed.

*

I am convinced that there is no cure for Rocky. He will be with us forever.

*

Ted Turner has put his foot in his mouth so many times over the years, his front teeth are starting to protrude.

*

Television weather forecasts would be better
if they told us things we didn't already
know, like why some idiots continue to jog
in this kind of weather, how long you can
remain in a cold shower before you begin
to wrinkle and shrink, and, speaking of
relative humidity, how much you perspire
while having sex with your cousin.

*

I'm going to learn to handle it when I
switch through the channels with my
remote-control device and discover *The
Newlywed Game* is still on the air and nobody
has shot Bob Eubanks.

*

What we fought the Revolutionary War about was putting those bloody kidney-pie-eating, wrong-side-of-the-road-driving blokes in their place, and here they were running the American music scene.

*

It all began with cosmetics commercials screaming at us on television. Our forefathers rallied behind "Fifty-four-forty or Fight!" and "Remember the Alamo!" and "A Chicken in Every Pot!" For this generation, it has been "The Wethead is Dead!"

Frankly, I don't care how some dockworker spells "relief" when he's got gas. He ought to have the decency to go on home when that happens, anyway.

Sports

One of the best things a man can do for his son is pass along a love for baseball.

*

Pulling for the Braves is like pulling for a Democratic nominee for president. It's your classic effort in futility.

*

Press-gate people not only put cats in laundromat dryers, they also probably have sex with pigs and made motorboat sounds in their soup as children.

*

As an Atlantan, I wish we could have kept the Braves our little secret, sort of like having an alcoholic uncle.

*

Relief pitchers in baseball are paid according to how many "saves" they have. Secretaries should be paid on the same basis for the number of times they save their bosses from embarrassing situations, such as being discovered as total incompetents.

*

I don't think anybody really likes the Yankees, not even the Yankees themselves. I think some people say they are Yankee fans only as a means of getting attention. I hate these people, too, and I hope they get constipated.

*

What George Steinbrenner has done is unforgivable: With him at the helm, it's not fun to hate the Yankees anymore. You just sort of feel sorry for them.

*

Rising star in women's golf or tennis: Any player with large breasts, thin legs, and a pretty face who hasn't had a lesbian affair yet.

*

Nothing in sports is quite as exciting as the moment the gate opens and all that tonnage of horseflesh bursts away with my financial future dependent upon which horse is in the biggest hurry.

*

Soccer breeds fan violence because it's very
dull, and when the fans get bored, they pass
the time by trying to maim and kill
one another.

*

Too many soccer teams wear dark socks
with their shorts, a violation of every
fashion law ever written.

*

Sports photos can be worn and tiresome.
Ever really look at a newspaper photograph
of a bunch of guys playing football? It
usually looks more like a big pile of laundry
than anything else.

*

Doing PR for the Falcons was a little like
doing PR for the Italian army during World
War II.

*

It is now possible to buy a copy of *Sports
Illustrated* and see a pair of women's breasts.
I knew when the American League adopted
the designated hitter rule, sports would
never be the same.

*

All this criticism about college sports and
the constant calls for reforms, I believe, is

rooted—and I firmly believe this—in the fact that all those former nerds, geeks, and lizards in high school and college are trying to get even.

*

Educate our athletes and most of them will quit playing ball and start hanging around playing video games with the other students.

*

There is hope. I read recently of a new study that indicates males who wear their trousers too tight can have very low sperm counts as a result, and have a difficult time fathering children. As tight as those bicycle pants are, there's a good chance this generation of pedalers may be the last.

*

I have never seen a polo match and neither has anyone I know.

*

I hate girls' basketball. Girls can't jump.

*

Unorganized Monster Trucking is where a couple of guys begin arguing who has the best Monster Truck. Then, to settle the issue, they go out and attach a chain to a couple of fast-food restaurants. The one who can pull his restaurant across town first is the winner.

*

Nobody has been able to find the abominable snowman because he's hiding from fifteen-year-old boys on skis.

*

The only thing uglier than a bowling shoe is Gloria Vanderbilt.

*

There's been a quarter of a century of Super Bowls, and most of them have had all the drama of the 1980 presidential election, when Ronald Reagan was pronounced the winner over Jimmy Carter before the two candidates even got up to shave on Election Day.

*

I am to golf what Muammar Qaddafi is to world peace.

*

I can make divots in which a small boy could get lost.

*

If the deer had guns too, then, and only
then, would hunting really be a sport.

*

If the players would attempt to beat each
other over the heads with their sticks, it
would improve hockey fighting a great deal
—that, or allow them to carry knives.

*

As we have proved with many of our
popular American sports, it is better to
have the violence on the field than in the
bleachers.

Fashion and Culture

Understand that I am usually a kind and gentle person. I am kind to animals, except cats, and I am gentle when it comes to children, unless they are screaming in the seat behind me on an airplane.

*

I call any dinner party where you have to say "Excuse me" when you burp fancy.

*

Anybody who says, "Have a nice one,"
"Hot enough for you?," "So how's the
wife?," or "You know" more than five
times in any sentence should cool
their heels in the slammer for a
few days.

*

I'm convinced that ties restrict the blood
flow to the brain, causing such disorders as
forgetfulness, blurred eyesight, and even
criminal tendencies. Al Capone was rarely
seen without a tie. The same goes,
incidentally, for Richard Nixon.

*

Take the sign that says NO SHIRT, NO SHOES, NO SERVICE. Does this mean that as long as I have on a shirt and shoes I can take off my pants and still get the bacon cheeseburger?

*

Jesus wore sandals, it is true. But he didn't wear those awful socks with them, and that's why New Jersey—especially Newark —turned out the way it did.

*

A man who wears socks the same color as his shorts is a bowler or builds cabinets in his basement or contributes to television evangelists.

*

I remain convinced that if the Lord had wanted men to wear socks, he never would have allowed Christian Dior to sell them for ten bucks a pair.

*

I predicted the coming of the leisure suit back in the late sixties. What led me to such a projection was the sudden falloff in the purchase of Nehru jackets, not to mention the fact that a group of geologists digging in the mountains of West Virginia discovered the world's richest vein of polyester.

*

If you must wear a tank top, at least make
certain you have a tattoo to go with it so
people will think you've been out to sea
since the mid-sixties and don't know
any better.

*

I have a rather small backside. There's
enough room in the seat of a pair of my
jeans for a small company of Chinese
soldiers to bivouac.

*

People who say "film" instead of "movie" usually attended a school without a good football team and don't think Joe Don Baker did a helluva job in the classic *Walking Tall*.

*

I never cared much for the artsy crowd. They are the kind of people who would look at a photograph or a painting of a cat nailed to a telephone pole and say, "My, look at those lines."

*

Hasn't just about everybody seen all that stuff in the Smithsonian by now? We could box it up and store it someplace, and if anybody wanted to look at it again, they would be welcome to, as long as they were willing to go through the boxes and pull it out themselves.

*

I don't have anything against anybody else chewing tobacco, but it's just not my cup of spit.

Money

This is America, we have a capitalistic society, and I like an occasional bottle of wine with a cork in it.

*

Yeah, I do write books because you get money for it. Otherwise, I wouldn't do it. Instead, I would get myself a job in a convenience store in Florida and steal lottery tickets.

*

I couldn't have afforded syrup if it had
fallen to three cents a sop.

*

I just want to make enough money to send
my dog to school so he can learn to read.

*

If my ex-wives and I formed a musical
group, we'd be Po' Boy and the
Alimonyettes.

*

That is how my generation found the good life. We borrow, and it doesn't bother us to owe up the wazoo.

*

Snuggle up to a fat girl when you go to sleep at night and think what you could save in insulation costs for your house.

*

I'm not saying my friend Rigsby often comes up with half-baked ideas that are supposed to make him a fortune and never do, but he's the same guy who tried to start a fast-food franchise that featured burger-on-a-rope.

*

If John Wayne were still alive, he'd know
what to do to the Japanese investors: take a
7 iron and run them and their checkbooks
back home before it's too late and Vanna
White has to learn eight zillion character
signs in the Japanese alphabet to keep
her job.

*

If you play golf, notice how many perfectly
good tees have been left on tee boxes. If
there are lots of them, then the economy
is fine.

Politics

Politicians are a lot like wild beasts.
Drugged, they're a lot less dangerous.

*

You don't mess with Charles Bronson,
Mother Nature, or the Constitution. Sooner
or later, they will all get revenge.

*

Watergate: The older I get, the more I think it was much ado about nothing other than a new breed of journalists running amok instead of covering fires.

*

I think Jimmy Carter would have been a lot better off as president if, when he moved to Washington, he'd told brother Billy to wait in the truck.

*

I wouldn't pee on Ted Kennedy's leg if he was on fire.

*

Atlanta mayor Maynard Jackson is a person of size. I'm not saying he's fat, or anything like that, but I will say when he steps on a cigarette, that sucker is out.

*

The first thing I would do as president of the New Confederacy is try to take Hilton Head Island, South Carolina, back from the Yankees.

*

A war between Oklahoma and Texas would be a lot of fun to watch on TV, I think.

*

The only good liberal is one who has been thrown out of office or is up in Alaska somewhere trying to save the whales and isn't around to get on my very last nerve.

*

It has occurred to me that if we continue putting forth efforts to save the whales, one of these days we're going to be up to our eyeballs in whales and I'll bet those things smell terrible.

*

Make a law against burning the flag in protest, and that could lead to a law against burning down a post office in protest of long lines, surly workers, and the fact you just received a nice birthday card from your grandmother, who died in 1962.

*

They say President Bush doesn't want to tax the rich. That's because he doesn't know anybody who isn't rich, and that wouldn't be a very nice way to treat your friends.

*

Tell the Japs if they try to sell one more Toyota, we're cranking up the *Enola Gay* again.

*

I figure we can make our own vodka, and there's nothing else in Name du Jour (formerly the Soviet Union) worth having.

*

We ought to keep the rich as rich as possible, because nobody poor was ever able to afford to give anybody else a job.

*

Iraqi president and minister of tourism Saddam Hussein (pronounced "who sane") was just kidding when he made that remark about plucking out our eyes. Insiders say President Hussein is a real jokester who is always talking about plucking out an eye or

two. It's his way of saying, "Come to
Iraq, mon."

*

The Saudis don't believe in beer. I'm not
certain such a country is worth defending,
even against Saddam Hussein.

*

Does Yasir Arafat have a brother
named Nosir?

*

Why do we need Congress itself? I think
we've just solved a huge portion of the

deficit problem here. Or, put it another way: Get a real job, Newt.

*

What this country has needed for a long time is to kick butt.

Health

If we listen to health-food advice, all we would be allowed to put in our stomachs would be something animals graze on, bee pollen, and various sorts of bran.

*

You smoke, you die. You drink, you die. You eat all that greasy food, you die. You don't jog, you don't aerobicize, you die. So one night you're sitting in your living room reading *Health and Prevention* magazine, and

radon gas comes in, goes right up your
butt, and kills you. Ha!

*

Maybe all of us should band together and
say "Enough is enough. Please don't tell us
what else will kill us."

*

Nonsmokers and smokers, I predict, will
have a civil war eventually and kill off great
numbers of both sides all in the name
of health.

*

A cigarette was like a little reward I gave
myself twenty-five to forty times a day.

*

I can deal with secondhand smoke, as long
as it's not coming from the roof of
my house.

*

I gave myself an out. I'm going to start
smoking again on my ninetieth birthday.

*

Worry kills, too. Would somebody please
mention that to the Surgeon General?

*

I doubt any studies have been done on such a thing, but I would wager that a great many crimes of passion have been committed because some guy's Jockey shorts have ridden up on a hot day and caused him great discomfort and his fuse to be greatly shortened.

*

When a person loses weight, where does the weight go? It has to go somewhere, doesn't it? One thought I've had is that when a person loses weight, it evaporates up into the atmosphere somewhere. Is there in fact a danger that Americans are losing so much weight these days the accumulated fat might all cling together up in the heavens and eventually block out the sun? Oprah lost enough weight by herself to block out several Ohio cities, not to mention all of Dade County, Florida.

*

We take so many pills in this country, there must be some pills for pill stress. I'd ask my doctor for some, but I'm afraid he would give them to me.

*

Undershorts that are too tight often are the cause of many maladies, such as migraine headaches, disco fever, and possibly even a sudden desire to adorn one's earlobe.

*

Secondhand Alcohol Breath: If you are on an airplane, for instance, and the person next to you is pouring down double scotches, you could get liver damage breathing this person's intoxicating exhales. The solution to this problem is to not allow Ted Kennedy on commercial flights.

*

Polyester Pollution: Most people have gotten the word by now that polyester leisure suits are tacky, and they are taking theirs out into the backyard and burning them. The fumes go into the atmosphere and turn the rain purple, and that's why we are getting such freaks of nature like Prince.

*

I am convinced ginger ale can heal the sick and raise the dead.

*

It takes a real man, I suppose, to stare death square in the eye. I think I'll go over to the Waffle House and drool.

A belt of all those things we like that we aren't supposed to enjoy anymore might do us all a world of good.

Travel

Natives of the Deep South know their way around snow much the same as a rhinoceros knows its way around roller skates.

*

I went to Rhode Island once, and it was very cold and none of the native women went around without their tops on. I can think of no reason to go back.

*

I can't think of anything that is sexy about the state of Indiana.

*

Put a tent over Los Angeles so whatever it is they breathe out there doesn't spread to the rest of the country.

*

There were always some suspicions on the part of those who grew up in the hinterlands that there really was no New York City. What if it was nothing but a clever hoax? What if *The Ed Sullivan Show* came to us from a warehouse on the outskirts of Greenville, South Carolina?

*

I know there's not a North Dakota. What you think is North Dakota is actually part of Canada, and it's so cold and bleak there the Canadians are trying to pass it off as a part of this country.

*

Most people who don't live in New York think of it as the home office for obnoxious behavior.

*

On a New York subway train you can get heavily fined if you spit. On the

other hand, you may throw up
for nothing.

*

You start lining up in front of street signs
to get your picture taken in New York City,
they know right away you parked your
turnip truck on Staten Island and took the
ferry across and you're some kind of
bumpkin or hick or geek or hillbilly, and a
taunting crowd will gather and tell you to
go back home.

*

The "Federation of Former New Jersey
Americans" miss such things as seeing

bodies floating in rivers. They meet at Barney's Waterslide every other Wednesday.

*

As to Minnesota, nobody really lives a long time there. It's so cold it just seems like it.

*

The Mormons are in charge of everything in Utah, including the state's liquor laws, which are so complex it's easier to drive to Wyoming to pick up a six-pack than it is to stay in Utah and try to figure out which day it's not against the law to order a vodka tonic if you're left-handed.

*

At least Canada fought on our side during World War II, and I will eventually get around even to forgiving them for introducing hockey to this country.

*

Ever notice the first thing you see at an airport? It's a big sign that says TERMINAL. Have a nice flight.

*

Given the choice, I will never fly, but given no choice, I will never fly sober.

*

I've never understood why the flight attendants take my drink away during both takeoffs and landings. That's when I need a drink the most.

*

Deliver me from the guy who's mad at his boss and is in charge of making certain all the bolts are tight for the flight to Omaha.

*

I had previously been afraid to drink on a flight because of how hard I had prayed it wouldn't crash. I was afraid if I sinned and had a drink, it would make God mad and He would crash the plane. Later, however, I realized if I had asked God what I should do to stop feeling terror on a plane, in all His infinite wisdom He would have said, "Have a couple of drinks."

*

Trains stay on the ground, as God intended. Remember: "Lo, I will be with you always." He never mentioned "high."

*

The only drawback to living a long time in Hawaii is you get very old and your eyesight

eventually goes, so you can no longer see
the young girls move their bodies, but you
still have to put up with all that
ukelele music.

*

I'm not certain where the world's behind
is, but Libya certainly would be one of my
first guesses. New Jersey wouldn't come
until much later.

*

Most Italian last names rhyme with
a vegetable.

*

Never fly an airline run by a country where a lot of its people worship cows.

*

I found another airline I wouldn't fly, as well—SwissAir. Their symbol is a red cross.

*

I bought a handy book on frequently used Arabic phrases such as *"Be-bop, fallah, gunga, arahmafungo,"* which means, "Me? An infidel? Heck no, and neither is my dog, Catfish—which is English for Mohammad."

*

If the women I saw were any indication of the beauty of the entire female population of the Soviet Union, Tammy Faye Bakker could walk down a street in Moscow and dogs wouldn't growl at her.

*

I suppose all this portrays me as a classic xenophobe. Actually, I'm not afraid of xenos. It's foreigners who frighten me.

*

If we all spoke the same, dressed the same, acted the same, thought the same, then this country would not be the unique place that it is, would not have the benefit of our spice and variety, and everybody probably would be in the Rotary Club.

Times Have Changed

Normally, I'm against most anything that is
supposed to be new and make my
life easier.

*

I've never been very good with machinery.
And machinery, in my mind, at least, is just
about anything you can't eat, wear, or read.

*

All those who are machinery-impaired like myself know that when all else fails, curse at whatever it is that is giving you a problem.

*

A shower with a mere trickle makes me consider joining a terrorist group.

*

If the workers at my post office had been Pony Express riders, the Indians could have caught them on foot.

*

My idea of camping out is being out of half-and-half for my coffee in the morning.

*

The filth they are selling as music these days isn't really music, just a guy with a deep voice saying a lot of dirty words while somebody beats on a barrel with a 2 iron and somebody else kills a cat in the background.

*

Perhaps if front porches came back and people started sitting on them again, we'd learn to relax more and talk to one another

more, and being bitten by a mosquito
would at least be some contact with nature.

＊

Some people spend a lot of money on
camping equipment and spend weeks in the
wilderness when they could save themselves
a lot of trouble simply by occasionally going
out in their backyards to pee.

＊

If we do venture out of our houses today,
it's usually to get in the hot tub.

＊

Today, parents are concerned about their children joining a religious cult or becoming a drug dealer. When I was growing up, they were worried about us putting an eye out.

*

Hey, we sent a man to the moon, and all we got was a few stupid rocks. If there's life on Uranus, they'll get in touch with us sooner or later.

*

What I really worry about when I think of writing something on a computer is, where does all that writing go when you push a button and it vanishes from the screen? Is it kept in a batch of wires in the back of the computer? Does it go to some central location in a vault buried underneath a Kmart in Fort Wayne, Indiana?

*

I don't want to awake one morning and find out I'm working for a computer, instead of the other way around.

*

There ought to be a law against computers writing letters to people.

*

Some of today's students spend a lot of time staring at computer screens. This fouls up their ability to see, as listening to loud music damages their hearing. When the teacher pulls down a map and explains where Mexico is located, they can't see the map, and they hear only a mumbling sound and think she's giving tomorrow's assignment, which is "Everybody go out and dye your hair orange."

*

Why doesn't anybody name a child "Norbert" or "Ernestine" anymore?

*

A woman at the Illinois corporate headquarters of McDonald's said the company has now served 75 billion hamburgers. Some quick arithmetic tells me that is about 300 hamburgers for every man, woman, and child in America and 2 million for Oprah Winfrey.

*

Not only do McDonald's personnel wear silly uniforms and hats, but Ronald McDonald is a disgrace to the clowning industry. He couldn't hold Clarabell's seltzer bottle.

*

Young men who wear their ball caps backward probably should carry a card around in their wallets that says, "If I have been injured and rendered unconscious, please don't try to turn my head around."

*

The Speech Police are on constant guard against remarks—humorous or otherwise—they consider to fall into those odious categories such as sexism, racism, xenophobia (the fear of foreigners), and homophobia (the fear of turning on Donahue and hearing guys complain because they can't get a marriage license and marry one another).

*

I'm forty-six, haven't forgiven the Japs for
Pearl Harbor, have tired of all of the
movements that just won't go away, still
don't want to be around homosexuals,
remain convinced Bernie Goetz did the
right thing when he shot those punks in the
New York subway, can quit smoking for a
time but can't seem to kick it for good,
have never drunk Perrier, still write on a
manual typewriter, can't figure out
telephones anymore, put too much vodka in
my screwdrivers, despise computers, and I
still don't have a clue what it is women
really want.

Religion

There's nothing like a good fight
among Baptists.

*

I remain convinced that if you live in the
Northeast and don't go to Sunday school,
when you die you go to Newark.

*

I'm sure it's in the Bible somewhere that instant grits are an unholy hybrid of the real thing.

*

You recall the Sixth Commandment. Moses tried to get God to forget it in the first place, but God didn't know at the time that the Playboy Channel would come along on cable and make everybody want to commit adultery.

*

I once saw faith healer Ernest Ainsley pray and a little girl who had one leg that was shorter than the other suddenly had legs of the same length, and she jumped up and did the jerk, right on the stage.

*

Did you hear Oral Roberts died? The check bounced.

*

I'm convinced humor is just as good for the soul as watching a television evangelist.

*

So what's Buddhism, a religion for fat people?

*

I'm predicting the world isn't going to come to an end anytime soon. There's too much unresolved, like whether or not Elvis is still alive, Jimmy Swaggart can stay on television, and if there will be another *Rambo* sequel.

*

I didn't have any out-of-body experiences. I had indeed seen a bright, beautiful light and had followed it, but it turned out to be a Kmart tire sale.

*

My friend Virgil couldn't have gotten through the Pearly Gates with a gold American Express card and written recommendations from three of the original disciples.

*

Let 'em scramble around trying to figure out what to do about my funeral. There was a bit of discomfort in getting me here, so there should be some hassle involved in sending me away.

*

As far as the End is concerned, I really don't think God will count off for drinking

beer. Tequila shooters, maybe. But
not beer.

*

For all my faults, I love my dog. Heaven's
got to be at least a little impressed
by that.

*

I just hope heaven doesn't run out of
Camels and fried chicken.